Images o

MW00633499

LGBT
HAMPTON ROADS

DR. CHARLES H. FORD AND
DR. JEFFREY L. LITTLEJOHN

ARCADIA
PUBLISHING

Copyright © 2016 by Dr. Charles H. Ford and Dr. Jeffrey L. Littlejohn
ISBN 978-1-4671-1613-8

Published by Arcadia Publishing
Charleston, South Carolina

Printed in the United States of America

Library of Congress Control Number: 2015951876

For all general information, please contact Arcadia Publishing:
Telephone 843-853-2070
Fax 843-853-0044
E-mail sales@arcadiapublishing.com
For customer service and orders:
Toll-Free 1-888-313-2665

Visit us on the Internet at www.arcadiapublishing.com

To the leaders and members of Hampton Roads Pride

CONTENTS

Acknowledgments   6

Introduction   7

1.   Before Stonewall in the Old Dominion:
      Pre-1969   9

2.   Mildly Militant:
      The Advent of Gay Liberation, 1969–1978   21

3.   Building and Sustaining Our Own Communities:
      1978–1988   33

4.   Triumph and Tragedy:
      Enduring the Plague Years, 1988–1998   43

5.   Treading Water in Transition:
      Our Own after *Our Own Community Press*, 1998–2007   55

6.   Renaissance and Transformation in the New Century:
      2007–2015   67

ACKNOWLEDGMENTS

This project began with Equality Virginia's Legends Committee of 2012; coauthor Charles H. Ford was on that committee and tasked with developing historical posters in reference to local LGBT history that could be displayed at the annual Legends Gala in November of that year. The research that went into that effort yielded a comprehensive time line, which went around the walls of the ballroom of the Norfolk Plaza Hotel where the gala was held. Key here in their support were Legends Committee cochairs Paul Meadors and Sarah Murphy and committee member Cheryl Scott of Deadline Digital Printing. Scott helped to design and display the time line posters. Then, these time line posters eventually morphed into even more developed and captioned posters, which were displayed as part of Hampton Roads Pride's History Experience in 2014 and 2015. Most helpful on Pride's History Committee to these efforts were Glen Coats, Jac Thomas, Kevin Pritchard, James Toy, and Connor Norton. Adam Law designed even larger displays, which attracted many festivalgoers to the history experience, which has become a permanent fixture of PrideFest.

Our Own Community Press was an invaluable resource in constructing our narrative, and we were graciously able to draw upon the whole run of issues held at the Old Dominion University Archives. Mel Frizzell of ODU Archives even donated a few of his photographs toward this effort. Similarly, at the Sargeant Room in Norfolk's Slover Library, librarian Troy Valos lent his considerable knowledge of the local area to guide our attempts to find suitable photographs. Local laypeople also heeded our call for images and information; most significant here were Jerry Halliday, Barry Moore, Scott Wyatt, Fred Osgood, Tony Wagerman, John Osterhout, and Laurel Quarberg.

We would also like to thank our title managers at Arcadia Publishing, Lily Watkins and Caitrin Cunningham, for their support and patience. This would be the first survey ever on this topic, and we are so glad that they saw the merit in our proposal. Finally, we would like to thank our long-suffering families and friends for once again helping us to execute another collaborative project.

INTRODUCTION

Lesbian, gay, bisexual and transgender (LGBT) people have always been present in Hampton Roads, Virginia, and long before many such people identified openly as such. The European, African, and Native American cultures that contributed to the making of Colonial Virginia featured various types of sexual and gender diversity, and even the British namesakes of important local towns, streets, and institutions were thought by contemporaries to defy traditional concepts of sexuality and gender identity. Our first chapter traces these origins and their development, noting the raucous maritime reputation of the region's centerpiece of Norfolk as "the wickedest city in America" by the 1890s. Indeed, Norfolk's reputation as a dirty, unhealthy place only solidified in the important years after the Civil War. The heavy concentration of saloons and taverns along the port city's harbor and in its downtown area was christened "Hell's Half-Acre" by New York observers. This rowdy patch resembled San Francisco's Barbary Coast and featured prostitutes of all shapes, sizes, and sexes. It would be the forerunner of the infamous East Main and Granby Streets dives that would distinguish Norfolk in the 20th century.

The world wars would further intensify that naughty and permissive image while dramatically increasing the population of all of the cities of Hampton Roads. Accordingly, identifiably LGBT communities begin to emerge in the region with the waves of young migrants from all over the nation. This increasing visibility could come in the most unlikely places, but it was met with periodic official oppression long after the Stonewall Riots in New York City in 1969. After World War II, Norfolk was known for its redevelopment; historic preservation came too little and too late to save much of its 19th-century architecture. But interestingly enough, the transition in the use of urban space was remarkably quite smooth for some of the most popular gay bars in the early 1970s and 1980s. These downtown establishments, which had been straight or heterosexual family places in preceding decades, changed gradually to a gay male clientele, largely with the same exact names and owners. Two Jewish brothers, for example, owned the Continental on 111 Tazewell Street; it was a premier jazz club in the 1950s and 1960s. By the 1970s, jazz no longer was bringing in the business, so the format changed to gay male. And then, the Continental was raided by Norfolk's police on January 28, 1978, and seven patrons were randomly arrested for frequenting a "bawdy house." Despite or maybe because of the bad publicity, the brothers kept their bar's name and their doors open, and then Tony Pritchard, owner of the College Cue Club, bought the Continental in early 1983, changing its name to the Boiler Room.

Our second chapter chronicles this growing presence as well as the founding of local LGBT institutions in the 1970s. In 1975, Leonard Matlovich, decorated Vietnam veteran and Georgia native, was the first enlisted serviceman to come out as gay before caught or accused by someone else. This he did as a technical sergeant deployed at Langley Air Force Base in Hampton. Matlovich was immediately thrown into the international media spotlight, and with the September 8, 1975, issue of *Time* magazine, he would become the first openly gay person on the cover of any major magazine with national circulation. Closer to home, Matlovich was assisted by bar owner Pritchard and the Unitarian Church, and his example seemed to embolden others to come out as well. His brief sojourn in Hampton Roads helped to jump-start the founding of *Our Own Community Press* and other LGBT infrastructure in 1976 and 1977, even if his case to stay in the Air Force dragged on long after he had left eastern Virginia for the freer air of San Francisco.

Our third chapter follows the building of LGBT infrastructure and the backlash against such growth during the 1980s. That backlash was quite real. Many people at the time were aware of the police harassment of gay men, whether in bars or public parks, but one should realize that such surveillance and monitoring also was used against local lesbians, whether civilian or military. As the longtime owner of the HerShee Bar (at Norfolk's Five Points), Annette Stone recounts that "12 public officials—most in full regalia and equipped with walkie-talkies and weapons—entered the bar a few hours after our grand opening" in early March 1983. Stone noted that at least three women were arrested that night, two of them for just using the men's room. And this government-sanctioned oppression of the HerShee apparently continued for a long time afterward with around 20 such shows of intimidating force each month.

Our fourth chapter notes the heavy impact of the HIV/AIDS epidemic as well as of continuing discrimination in the late 1980s to the end of the century. The hope for a better future for local LGBT peoples was temporarily dashed, as the AIDS pandemic hit Hampton Roads hard. Tony Pritchard, among others, however, pitched in to found the Tidewater AIDS Crisis Taskforce (TACT) in 1983, and other AIDS service organizations emerged and merged by the early 21st century to form a robust addition to the local safety net of social welfare.

Our fifth chapter delves into the difficult years of transition after the region lost its own LGBT newspaper in 1998. At the turn of the century, LGBT Hampton Roads seemed to have had lost key infrastructure from the liberation era (*Our Own Community Press* had closed, bars came and went), and its Pride celebrations remained rather limited affairs for the region's size. Marriage equality seemed less and less likely with the passage of the Marshall-Newman Amendment of 2006, and the area's LGBT organizations and allied businesses seemed to be either perpetually at odds or in isolation from each other. Then, luckily, those gloomy prospects seemed to change.

Our sixth and last chapter celebrates the rebirth of energy and activism that seemed to begin with the founding of Hampton Roads Business Outreach (HRBOR) in June 2007. HRBOR, the de facto LGBT Chamber of Commerce, has built bridges and allowed for possibilities that no one would have thought possible; it has permitted a new visibility that transcends the old chasms between assimilationists and activists. And, in its wake, new leaders, partnerships, and organizations have formed—to the point where HRBOR has joined the Peninsula Chamber of Commerce. Furthermore, one of the most momentous turning points in the development of LGBT Hampton Roads was the bringing of PrideFest to center stage at Town Point Park in June 2011. This ambitious decision dramatically increased the scope and reach of the event and has strengthened the relationships between our own communities and civic agencies.

While promoting economic growth, LGBT peoples have been key in the making of cultural institutions. The Boston marriage of Irene Leache and Anna Wood bequeathed extraordinary cultural legacies to Hampton Roads, and that yield began with their school for well-to-do white girls, the Leache-Wood Seminary, which stood at the corner of Granby and Freemason Streets from 1871 to 1901. The school then moved to Fairfax Avenue in Ghent (away from the bars) after the death of Irene Leache in 1900, but Anna Wood (who would die at age 90 in 1940) would go on to establish the Irene Leache Memorial, out of which came the Norfolk Museum of Arts and Sciences, the forerunner of today's Chrysler Museum of Art. The memorial also contributed to the founding of the Little Theatre, the Norfolk Symphony Orchestra, and other gems in the port city. In turn, Walter P. Chrysler Jr., the heir to a considerable automotive fortune, helped to turn the obscure third-rate Norfolk Museum of Arts and Sciences into the world-class Chrysler Museum of Art of today. He also happened to be a semi-closeted gay man, who had moved to Norfolk in the early 1970s for good (back to the hometown of his second wife, Jean Outland Chrysler) from the rather lavender resort of Provincetown, Massachusetts. But his money, talent, and connections outweighed any personal indiscretions in the minds of the most of the city's oligarchy, and they generally welcomed him without reservations. In general, then, LGBT folks have had a significant impact upon both the high- and low-brow scenes in Hampton Roads from the get-go.

One

BEFORE STONEWALL IN THE OLD DOMINION
PRE-1969

The cultures of early Hampton Roads, Virginia, were sprightly mixtures of Native American, European, and African mores, and all of these contributing cultures had what would today be called LGBT dimensions. For instance, as a way of showing appreciation for bountiful crops in the autumn, women of Powhatan's Confederacy donned male garb and danced around a fire in the middle of their capital, singing sexually explicit songs and confounding English explorers such as John Smith. In many parts of central and western Africa, the best summoners of the divine were women, but men living as women were perfectly acceptable. In western Europe, Christianity was officially against any kind of gender-bending and associated androgyny with witchcraft, but the sailing culture that facilitated the Age of Discovery also brought with it cross-dressing traditions and same-sex desires.

As "America's first region," Hampton Roads has many places whose namesakes happen to be English royals within what would today be called the LGBT spectrum. Jamestown, the first permanent English settlement in the New World, was named for James I of England, who, while married with children, had several male lovers. Princess Anne of Princess Anne County and Road was the daughter of King James II and eventually became Queen Anne in 1702. She endured 17 pregnancies via her husband George of Denmark, but she did find the most solace in especially strong female friendships, particularly with Sarah Churchill, Duchess of Marlborough.

Norfolk emerged as the metropolitan center of Hampton Roads by the 19th century, and its reputation as an especially dirty, permissive, and rowdy place only seemed to solidify with the passing years. In fact, the heavy concentration of saloons and taverns resembled San Francisco's Barbary Coast and featured prostitutes of all shapes, sizes, and sexes. It would be the forerunner of the infamous East Main and Granby Streets dives that would distinguish Norfolk in the 20th century. By the 1960s, neighboring Princess Anne County and then the new city of Virginia Beach had its own LGBT expressions with Craig's, a gay male bar, which was raided and closed for same-sex dancing on its premises in March 1965. Yet LGBT contributions were not always geared toward nightlife; in particular, the female couples of educators Irene Leache and Anna Wood and activists Bertha Douglas and Ione Diggs helped to raise the cultural bar in the sailors' mecca.

Pictured here is John Smith's map of Virginia, which features Native American images of power and prestige. Based on Smith's travels throughout the Chesapeake region, the map highlights the geographic features of the area. The bird serpent headdress on the figure in the upper right-hand corner was interpreted by Europeans to be androgynous and thus evil. (Courtesy of the Library of Congress.)

Indeed, Powhatan's priests (or shamans) had a much different world view than the invading English—one in which people listened intently even to people with whom they disagreed, in which women had more sway and say, and in which cross-dressing was a normal part of certain rituals. All of these differences were deemed by the English to be signs of weakness and inferiority. (Courtesy of Virtual Jamestown.)

Contrary to English propaganda, the Powhatan Confederacy was civilized. Local inhabitants lived in villages like Pomeiock, depicted here in a John White watercolor. For their part, the Powhatan leaders saw the English as incompetent and effete men who could not feed themselves, with the Kecoughtans, in particular, making fun of the English during the starving times. Masculinity was contested on both sides in the initial encounters. (Courtesy of Virtual Jamestown.)

The towne of Pomeiock and true forme of their howses, couered and enclosed some wᵗʰ matts, and some wᵗʰ barcks of trees. All compassed abowt wᵗʰ smale poles stock thick together in stedd of a wall.

West Africans, who first arrived in Virginia in 1619, brought with them beliefs, gods, and rituals that contrasted significantly with the official Christianity of the English. In many parts of West Africa, the best summoners of the divine were women, but men living as women were perfectly acceptable as priests. (Courtesy of Wikimedia.)

11

At Jamestown, homosexual expressions of affinity were forbidden by law. In 1624, cabin boy William Couse accused his captain, Richard Cornish, of forcibly sodomizing him. Cornish was hanged, on the governor of Virginia's orders, but his name lives on with the Richard Cornish Endowment Fund for Gay and Lesbian Resources at the College of William and Mary. (Courtesy of the Sidney E. King Collection, National Park Service.)

In 1629, the residents of Warraskoyak were preoccupied with the sexual identity of indentured servant Thomas Hall, who changed gender with different jobs and sexual partners. Hall's case landed in Jamestown's Quarter Court, which ruled that Hall was both a man and a woman. The court sentenced Hall to wear both male and female clothes in order to provoke public ridicule. (Courtesy of the Sidney E. King Collection, National Park Service.)

In Britain, Christianity forbade gender-bending and associated androgyny with witchcraft. Yet visible subcultures of men who loved men surfaced anyway. The 18th-century "molly" pictured here in the 1772 Carington Bowles print *How D'Ye Like Me* had a long pedigree of similarly effeminate brothers and sisters from previous centuries. (Courtesy of the British Museum.)

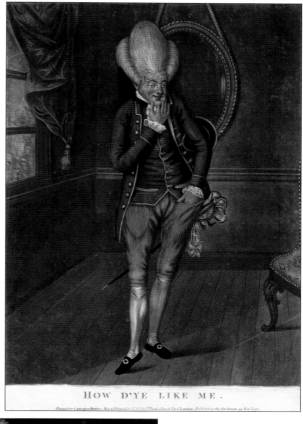

HOW D'YE LIKE ME.

Virginia was born with issues of gender identity. Its namesake was Elizabeth I of England, the purported virgin queen, pictured here in the famous *Armada Portrait* (1588). In the 1580s, Sir Walter Raleigh had called the region after a Native American "king," Wingina, but Elizabeth made sure that this land was named after her most prominent quality to contemporaries—her choice to remain single. (Courtesy of Wikimedia.)

One of the investors in the Virginia Company was Henry Wriothesley, the third Earl of Southampton, depicted here. He worked so hard to keep the venture of Virginia afloat that his title was the namesake for the harbor and region of Hampton Roads. A decade before that, he was the patron and reputed crush of William Shakespeare. In the 1590s, the Bard of Avon dedicated several sonnets to Wriothesley. (Courtesy of Wikimedia.)

The namesake of Jamestown was James I of England. Deemed "the wisest fool in Christendom" for his ability to achieve sectarian balance and relative peace, James was married to Princess Anne of Denmark. In addition to his marriage, he also had very strong emotional and probably sexual ties to certain young men at his court, such as the handsome George Villiers, the Duke of Buckingham. (Courtesy of Wikimedia.)

William III of England, pictured here, married his first cousin Mary, the eldest daughter of James II of England, in 1677. A decade later, the English Parliament deposed James in favor of William and Mary in the Glorious Revolution. Later, however, supporters of James conspired to reverse history, and they pointed to William's seemingly intimate relationships with young male courtiers as proof of his illegitimacy as ruler. (Courtesy of Wikimedia.)

Princess Anne, the namesake of Princess Anne County, was the daughter of James II of England; she eventually became Queen Anne in 1702. She endured 17 pregnancies via her husband, George of Denmark, but she did find the most solace in especially strong female friendships—most notably, with Sarah Churchill, the Duchess of Marlborough, and then, after breaking with Sarah, Abigail Masham. (Courtesy of Wikimedia.)

Grace Sherwood (whose recent commemorative statue by Robert G. Cunningham is featured here) seemed to be the conventional wife of a late 17th-century yeoman farmer in Princess Anne County (today's Virginia Beach), but she became the focus of persistent witchcraft allegations. Grace was an assertive mother and widow who dressed like a man while farming; she did not get along with her neighbors, who probably wanted her land for their own. These neighbors used Grace's admitted knowledge of herbal medicines to get local magistrates to make her go through the medieval trial by ordeal: she was ducked into Lynnhaven River, and that area still features a Witchduck Road. Even though Grace floated to the surface—which meant she was guilty of witchcraft—she was eventually released and lived to 80. (Courtesy of Charles H. Ford.)

In 1779, Gov. Thomas Jefferson made reforming Virginia's penal code a priority. While reducing the severity of sentencing for property crimes, Jefferson deemed sodomy as one of those awful behaviors that could still be harshly punished. Indeed, Jefferson's reform committee recommended castration for men and nose mutilation for women. The legislature never passed this suggestions, however, and sodomy remained a capital offense. (Courtesy of Wikimedia.)

John Laurens of South Carolina served the United States as both soldier and diplomat. Although married, he loved Lt. Colonel Alexander Hamilton, a fellow aide-de-camp under Gen. George Washington. At Yorktown, in 1781, the two friends—Laurens and Hamilton—turned lovers and helped to win the war together. Laurens was killed at the Battle of the Combahee River, near Charleston, less than a year later. (Courtesy of Wikimedia.)

Alexander Hamilton of New York was born out of wedlock in the Caribbean, but after service in the Revolutionary War, he became the first American secretary of the treasury. Hamilton liked both men and women, and although later married to Elizabeth Schuyler, he had an intense relationship with his friend and lover John Laurens. Hamilton was later killed in a duel with Aaron Burr. (Courtesy of Wikimedia.)

Stephen Decatur, the famed naval hero of the early American republic, married the daughter of the mayor of Norfolk, Susan Wheeler, in 1806. This marriage, though, was never a tightly knit partnership in part because of Decatur's long tours of duty and in part because of his strong emotional (and possibly physical) attachment to his best friend and fellow midshipman Richard Somers. (Courtesy of the Naval History and Heritage Command.)

Anna Wood, a founder of the Leache-Wood Seminary for girls, is seated in a reclining chair for this 1910 photograph of the school's theatrical ensemble. Wood's intimate friendship with Irene Leache had launched the school in downtown Norfolk in 1871. Anna also helped to found the Little Theatre, Norfolk Symphony, and the Norfolk Museum of Arts and Sciences. (Courtesy of the Sargeant Memorial Room at Norfolk Public Library.)

Dr. Raymond A. Vonderlehr (seated center), assistant surgeon general of the United States, is pictured here visiting a clinic for African Americans with syphilis located on East Bute Street in Norfolk in 1938. The woman meeting with him is teacher and activist T. Ione Diggs, whose longtime companion was attorney Bertha Douglas, the first African American woman to have a law firm in Hampton Roads. (Courtesy of the Sargeant Memorial Room at Norfolk Public Library.)

The Navy YMCA at 130 Brooke Avenue in downtown Norfolk offered a dormitory and recreational facilities for men, both civilian and military. Pictured here are two sailors in 1950 in its lobby. This YMCA, like its counterparts in other major cities, also inadvertently brought together gay and bisexual men who might have never met otherwise. (Courtesy of the Sargeant Memorial Room at Norfolk Public Library.)

Many midcentury Virginia Beach nightspots, such as the Surf Club (pictured), enforced a strict boy-girl policy when it came to dancing. But Craig's Restaurant on Atlantic Avenue allowed same-sex dancing, and it was the scene of a police raid on March 21, 1965. That night, 86 men were arrested, and their names were published in the *Virginia Beach Sun*. (Courtesy of the Sargeant Memorial Room at Norfolk Public Library.)

Man Dies In Woman's Clothes

Policeman Cleared In Death Of Sex Pervert

By FRANCIS H. MITCHELL

NORFOLK—The lurid career of Rufus Emerson, known sex pervert, was formally brought to a close in Norfolk police court Thursday, when a homicide charge against Officer William R. Robinette, who killed him, was dismissed.

Even more strange than some of his exploits, was the chain of circumstances that led to Emerson's death.

AND EVEN AFTER he lay dead in Southall's Lane on the night of June 11, his ambition was disclosed by identification he carried listing him as "colored, female."

According to police, a cab driver spotted Emerson in the 700 block of Granby street, clad in pedal-pushers and a blouse, calling to sailors in a loud voice, "come on, baby." The driver, identified as Mr. Lewis, testi-fied that he could not tell whether the person he saw was a male or female.

*   *   *

LEWIS TESTIFIED that he drove down to City Hall avenue and told Officer Robinette about the commotion on Granby street. The officer accompanied him back to the scene and attempted to place Emerson under arrest, he said.

Officer Robinette testified that when he got to the scene, Emerson stuck his head and shoulders through the door, grabbed him by his privates, and when he felt the pistol which he carried, released him.

*   *   *

THE POLICEMAN said he showed Emerson his shield and told him he was under arrest, whereupon Emerson ran toward the Post Office parking lot. He said that Emerson threw a brick at him, hit him with a board, and threatened to "cut his guts out." He testified that the chase went from Granby street to York street, then to Brewer street and into Southall's Lane, where he approached Emerson again and was threatened.

*   *   *

THE OFFICER said that he had been scratched, his shirt almost torn from his back, and his pocket while he threatened him. At this point, the officer told the Court, he pulled his revolver and when Emerson started to run again, shot him.

The cab driver, who first took the policeman to the scene, denied having taken sailors to the Granby street area which Emerson frequented, and denied going for an officer because he was "peeved" with the pervert.

*   *   *

By the 1950s, downtown Norfolk had a well-entrenched reputation for having prostitutes of every size, shape, orientation, and gender, and Rufus Emerson, described here, was not unusual. What was unfortunately predictable, however, was the casual and approved violence against a LGBT person in which his or her life was considered expendable because of a perceived perversion. Emerson died in part for being different. (Courtesy of the *Norfolk Journal and Guide*.)

Two

MILDLY MILITANT
THE ADVENT OF GAY LIBERATION,
1969–1978

The emergence of identifiably lesbian, gay, bisexual, and transgender communities in Hampton Roads happened during and after World War II, as migrants from all over the country came there and settled due to their military service. Local businesses began to take notice. For instance, Mickey's in downtown Norfolk provided an internationally known respite for sailors and their friends during the height of the Cold War, but by the 1970s, it had acquired a largely gay male clientele. In 1972, Mickey's even spawned the first local gay newspaper—*Friends*—in the area, edited by Jerry Halliday and H.T. Kelly Jr. It lasted four issues in tabloid format and featured the advertisements of some Granby Street shops.

The police also noticed this burgeoning movement, and they did everything to suppress it. The Gay Freedom Movement of Tidewater (GFMT) began with an August 1972 meeting of 300 "known homosexuals" and one undercover cop apparently at a "local Norfolk church." A Virginia Department of Alcoholic Beverage Control (ABC) Board investigation of an amateur production of *The Boys in the Band* at the College Cue Club had deemed the performance obscene, and that decision unleashed waves of police harassment that summer and fall, which whittled the turnout for the GFMT down to about 50 people. Indeed, raids of LGBT bars in Hampton Roads would continue well into the 1980s.

The Leonard Matlovich story reenergized local activism a few years later. Matlovich, decorated Vietnam veteran and Georgia native, identified himself as gay *before* being caught in a sexual act or being accused of homosexuality by someone else. This unprecedented transparency placed him on the front cover of none other than the September 8, 1975, issue of *Time* magazine. The Matlovich story prompted many local men and women to come out of the closet, and it also helped to inspire the forming of the Unitarian Church of Norfolk's Gay and Lesbian Caucus, whose monthly newsletter eventually became *Our Own Community Press*. Other LGBT infrastructure such as the local chapter of the Metropolitan Community Church (MCC) emerged in 1976 and 1977, which, in turn, helped to fuel the Anita Bryant protests that changed "mildly militant" Tidewater forever.

Mickey's Tavern on Brooke Street in downtown Norfolk was conveniently located near the Navy YMCA. This contributed to its largely military and later gay clientele. The tavern featured drinks, dancing, and nightlife, which attracted men and women from the city and its environs. Uniform and gear shops surrounded the bar, which spawned a gay newsletter in 1972. (Courtesy of the Sargeant Memorial Room at Norfolk Public Library.)

The owners of Mickey's gradually transitioned their format from purely naval to gay male in the late 1960s and early 1970s. This was done largely as the city lost population to the suburbs, and the bar owners were keen to find any new patrons. Gay men were thought to have disposable income and were overrepresented in preservation and renovation efforts. (Courtesy of the Sargeant Memorial Room at Norfolk Public Library.)

The 1970s brought a greater visibility to the long-standing red-light districts west of and alongside Granby Street in downtown Norfolk. Pictured here are an ostensibly heterosexual massage parlor and adult bookstore on West Tazewell Street in 1973. Village Books, however, would be one of the first places to sell homosexual erotica in the city without fear of violating obscenity laws. (Courtesy of the Sargeant Memorial Room at Norfolk Public Library.)

The Paddock, located at 125 Plume Street, was a longtime family restaurant in the downtown area. Like many of its nearby counterparts, the restaurant turned into a gay male bar by the late 1970s. Its specialty was the leather and Levis subculture, which romanticized props of masculinity such as leather jackets or construction boots. (Courtesy of the Sargeant Memorial Room at Norfolk Public Library.)

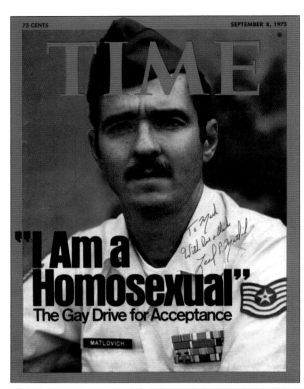

Leonard Matlovich, a decorated Vietnam veteran and native of Georgia, was a regular at the College Cue Club before he became an international icon of gay liberation. His brief sojourn in Hampton Roads stimulated local activism and visibility, especially after he was featured on the cover of *Time* magazine. (Courtesy of *Time*.)

The Unitarian church in Norfolk has long been an engine for civil rights and social justice causes. In the 1970s, gay liberation became one of the church's many causes. Leonard Matlovich's coming out prompted the church to take a large role in the struggle, and its gay and lesbian caucus launched a newsletter that became *Our Own Community Press* in 1976. (Courtesy of Norfolk Unitarian Church.)

Willard Frank was a key straight ally who fostered the Norfolk Unitarian Church's activist bent. Frank, a professor of history at Old Dominion University, had opposed massive resistance and supported public school desegregation during the 1950s. Later, he became a vocal supporter of gay rights. The Franks worked alongside such LGBT stalwarts as Joseph McKay, Jayr Ellis, Jim Early, and Garland Tillery. (Courtesy of the Old Dominion University Archives.)

Tony Pritchard (pictured here at the 2006 PrideFest) opened the College Cue Club in 1971, and he supported early local efforts to gain legal and social equality for LGBT people in Hampton Roads. He would later go on to found other LGBT infrastructure, including Pride picnics and the Tidewater AIDS Crisis Taskforce. (Courtesy of Barry Moore.)

Anita Bryant was a popular singer and a spokesperson for Florida orange growers. She had been raised in rural Oklahoma and never questioned the conservative values of her upbringing. She had several Top 40 hits in the 1960s and was a well-known television personality by the 1970s. This made her a desirable advocate for those who opposed gay rights. (Courtesy of the *Virginian-Pilot* Archives.)

In her campaigns, Anita Bryant always emphasized what she believed were the adverse effects of gay liberation on children. That is why children played a prominent role in her performances, like the one pictured here at the Scope in Norfolk in June 1977. In Florida, she supported efforts to fire gay public school teachers for perversion and became a national spokeswoman against gay rights. (Courtesy of the *Virginian-Pilot* Archives.)

Here, with a group onstage, Anita Bryant portrays herself as one of many of the so-called silent majority of Americans who opposed unnatural cultural changes, such as gay liberation. Nevertheless, in 1980, she divorced her husband of 20 years, drawing fire for being a hypocrite, as divorce had been traditionally taboo. (Courtesy of the *Virginian-Pilot* Archives.)

Here, along Norfolk's Granby Street in Norfolk, protesters were on their way to the Scope to demonstrate against Anita Bryant's visit to Hampton Roads. This protest drew a wide array of interest groups, including Richmond gays and local Quakers. The protesters pictured here carry signs reading "Gay and Straight Unite and Fight All Forms of Bigotry" and "Stop Anita Bryant – Smash Gay Oppression!" (Courtesy of the *Virginian-Pilot* Archives.)

In response to Anita Bryant's repeated invocations of scripture, protesters emphasized that gay people could also be religious. "God Loves Us Too," declares one large sign at the front of this group of marchers. Other signs highlight "Gay Pride Day" and regional councils on human relations. (Courtesy of the *Virginian-Pilot* Archives.)

Anita Bryant had local support in Hampton Roads, as evidenced by this group outside of Scope. Here, a local minister reads from scripture while a small group of pro-Bryant activists hold signs reading "Repent and Be Saved, "Gays are Godless," and "Sinners not Sickness." (Courtesy of the *Virginian-Pilot* Archives.)

The Continental had been a jazz club during the 1950s and 1960s, when its torch singers picked up an increasingly gay male audience. In January 1978, it was the scene of a police raid in which seven men were arrested for same-sex dancing. In 1983, it would be taken over by Tony Pritchard and renamed the Boiler Room. (Courtesy of the Sargeant Memorial Room at Norfolk Public Library.)

Dr. Franklin Kameny of Washington, DC, who was the most famous victim of the Lavender Scare—the purging of gay federal employees during the Cold War—spoke at the Unitarian church on January 17, 1978. A donation of $1 was requested. Kameny then returned to Norfolk in early February for a workshop sponsored by the Norfolk Council on Human Rights. (Courtesy of the *Washington Post*.)

Gay and lesbian Catholics in Norfolk launched their own Dignity chapter in 1977. Pictured here are some of the members of that group. In January 1978, Dignity held a retreat for both gay men and lesbians in Richmond, and they were able to meet without papal disapproval locally until 1987. (Courtesy of Scott Wyatt.)

Walter P. Chrysler Jr. (left), pictured here with Andy Warhol, was the heir to an automotive fortune and helped to turn the third-rate Norfolk Museum of Arts and Sciences into the world-class Chrysler Museum of Art. He was also a semi-closeted gay man, who moved to Norfolk (to live with his second wife, Jean Outland Chrysler) from the lavender resort of Provincetown, Massachusetts. (Courtesy of the Chrysler Museum of Art.)

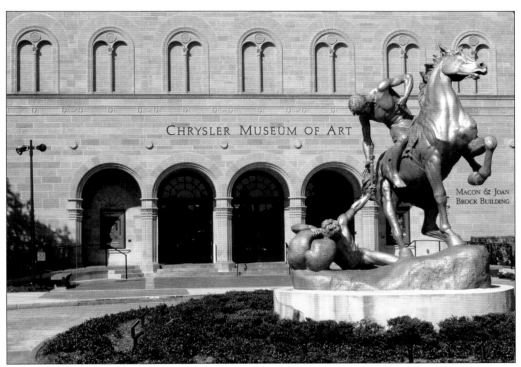

The Chrysler Museum of Art in Norfolk houses world-class collections in art and glass. Following in the tradition of its great benefactor, Walter P. Chrysler Jr., the museum has gradually become a key partner in the fight for LGBT people to gain respectability and identity. (Courtesy of the Chrysler Museum of Art.)

Artist Jack Whitlow brought dignity and respectability to representations of masculinity and the male nude in Hampton Roads, representations that mainstream standards had largely relegated to the margins of expression. His many drawings and images continue to adorn homes and warm hearts, just as when they were advertised in the pages of *Our Own Community Press* in the late 1970s. (Courtesy of the Old Dominion University Archives.)

Drag performances emerged in Hampton Roads during the 1890s, contributing to Norfolk's reputation as "the wickedest city in America." An especially vibrant and creative time for local drag shows, however, coincided with the heyday of the House of Camelot, which frequently held its events at the Golden Triangle Motor Hotel, now the Wyndham Garden Hotel, during the 1960s and 1970s. (Courtesy of the Sargeant Memorial Room at Norfolk Public Library.)

Three

BUILDING AND SUSTAINING OUR OWN COMMUNITIES
1978–1988

The local activism in Hampton Roads was quite impressive. One of the forerunners to Virginians for Justice (which is now Equality Virginia) was the Virginia Coalition for Lesbian and Gay Rights, which held its inaugural meeting in Richmond on February 24, 1978. The Hampton Roads delegation was the largest at the Richmond meeting, reflecting the energy and momentum begun by the Matlovich case just three years before. Indeed, Hampton Roads would dominate statewide advocacy platforms until well into the 1980s, in stark contrast to its later reputation as a provincial backwater.

Local nightlife blossomed in the late 1970s and 1980s as visibility continued to increase. New bars came and went, mainly in Norfolk yet also on the peninsula and in Virginia Beach. The Continental, an old jazz club turned gay male bar and the scene of a famous bar raid in January 1978, eventually became Tony Pritchard's Boiler Room. For women, Shirley's, the HerShee Bar, and then Stella Street, among others, sufficed. Beyond the bar scene, religious and collegiate groups solidified. Sports teams and leagues emerged. Communities had arisen.

The success of Hampton Roads in building LGBT infrastructure helped it to be the place in which national standards of obscenity were defined. Courts had given local communities wide discretion in suppressing speech or text that a majority of "reasonable" citizens might find pornographic. Accordingly, into the 1980s, local public libraries—most famously, in Virginia Beach—and other establishments (such as Thomas Nelson Community College in Hampton) refused to distribute copies of *Our Own Community Press* simply because of its use of the words gay and lesbian. In fact, local police, using this dragnet of oppression, harassed seemingly innocent and random patrons of gay bars with persistent raids long after the famous Stonewall rebellion in New York in 1969. In 1982, authorities attempted to seize the film *Taxi zum Klo* before it could be shown at the Naro Expanded Cinema in Norfolk's Ghent neighborhood. Community standards did change—but only through further court and political action. By the end of the 1980s, raids and controversies over simple identification became more the exception rather than the norm.

When the publishers of *Our Own Community Press* attempted to share the newspaper with venues outside of Norfolk, leaders in Virginia Beach resisted the effort. In March 1980, the Virginia Beach city manager decided to prevent the distribution of *Our Own Community Press*, and in April the city's library board restricted access to just one copy per month. (Courtesy of the Virginia Beach Public Library.)

Port cities provided the test cases for the legal interpretations of obscenity. Courts had given local communities discretion in suppressing material that a majority of "reasonable" citizens might find prurient. In 1982, the film *Taxi zum Klo* was seized temporarily by Norfolk police before it could be eventually shown at the Naro Expanded Cinema in Ghent. Community standards did change, however, through further court and political action. (Courtesy of Army Arch.)

This German film ironically was considered too artsy by aficionados of gay male pornography, but to local officials it was the worst of the worst when it came to sexual materials. The last X-rated film that the theater screened for public viewing, *Taxi zum Klo* was shown once at the Naro after a bitter court fight. (Courtesy of Wikimedia.)

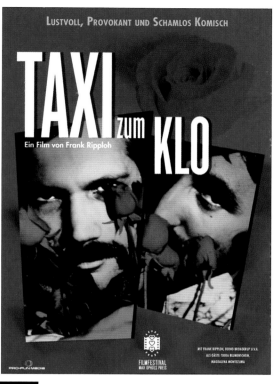

Vito Russo (pictured), author of *The Celluloid Closet*, spoke at the Unitarian church on May 8, 1982; psychiatrist Dr. Robert Scott of Riverview was the organizer. Scott arranged many stimulating lectures for local audiences, and he was one of the first people in the region to discuss HIV/AIDS prevention. (Courtesy of Wikimedia.)

The local mainstream reaction to the first wave of gay liberation was largely one of resigned indifference, but even centrist politicians found in LGBT cultures wedge issues to show solidarity with social conservatives who were unhappy with the cultural changes brought on by the 1960s. For example, local congressmen Paul Trible (pictured) and William Whitehurst, moderate Republicans, proudly voted to prohibit legal assistance to victims of gay discrimination in June 1981. (Courtesy of the *Daily Press*.)

Anti-LGBT bigotry was not restricted to Republicans over a generation ago. It enlivened a Democratic primary for state delegate in Norfolk in September 1982 between two redistricted incumbents. Thomas W. Moss (future Speaker of the Virginia House and Norfolk treasurer) loudly disavowed support from the pro-gay Mandamus Society in September 1982, while his opponent, Edythe Harrison, tried to ignore gay-rights advocacy altogether. Moss (right) is pictured talking with Norfolk councilman Anthony Burfoot. (Courtesy of the *Virginian-Pilot*.)

Doyle M. Levy, a teacher at Booker T. Washington High School, was murdered in February 1983. His body was found at the Surf Motel in Ocean View with multiple stab wounds and a slashed throat. Gregory Schroeder, a married 19-year-old Marine lance corporal, was charged with the slaying. Schroeder pled guilty in a case that focused on gay-bashing and robbery. (Courtesy of the Sargeant Memorial Room at Norfolk Public Library.)

In the 1970s, Freemason Street became a preferred spot for gay male cruising. Unaccompanied men walked from the bars downtown to meet other men in what they considered a "good" neighborhood. In 1983, Freemason residents forced the Norfolk Police Department to upgrade its presence in the area. The cruising then moved to other areas and later, the Internet. (Courtesy of the Sargeant Memorial Room at Norfolk Public Library.)

HERSHEE'S

FREE TO BE ME

NEAR AND FAR
WHERE THE WOMEN ARE!

DJ 7 NITES A WEEK

6117 Sewells Point Road Norfolk, VA
(804) 853-9842

Annette Stone launched the HerShee Bar at its longtime location in Norfolk's working-class Norview neighborhood in 1983. Its location brought LGBT visibility out of its usual areas of downtown or artsy Ghent and as a result was targeted by police for harassment and oppression. Nevertheless, the first openly gay person to run for city council in Norfolk launched her campaign here on December 8, 1983. (Courtesy of the Old Dominion University Archives.)

Charades in Virginia Beach deployed the artistic skills of Jack Whitlow in this mid-1980s advertisement for a holiday event in *Our Own Community Press*. It pushed the envelope for what could be printed, foreshadowing the serious debates over the proper display of nudity in the paper in the upcoming decade. (Courtesy of the Old Dominion University Archives.)

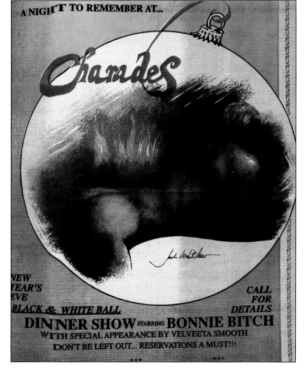

A NIGHT TO REMEMBER AT...

Charades

NEW
YEAR'S
EVE
BLACK & WHITE BALL

CALL
FOR
DETAILS

DINNER SHOW STARRING BONNIE BITCH
WITH SPECIAL APPEARANCE BY VELVEETA SMOOTH
DON'T BE LEFT OUT... RESERVATIONS A MUST!!!

Burma Poole was a frequent disc jockey at the popular College Cue Club. Her Top 10 hits for August 1983 included No. 1 "She Works Hard for the Money" by Donna Summer, but she played a wide variety of music ranging from new wave to rock and roll. (Courtesy of Burma Poole)

Torch singer Arnyce Anders (left) was a loyal muse to many local gay men in the 1970s and 1980s. She starred in a quite a few cabaret evenings, enlivening the roles of Mama Rose and Dolly Levi. She and her voice were literally larger than life. The men in the photograph are unidentified. (Courtesy of Carlton Hardy.)

Jerry Halliday became more of an entertainer than advocate by the Reagan era, but his comedy always had a political edge at the Cue. Here is an advertisement in *Our Own Community Press* for one of his puppeteering performances. (Courtesy of the Old Dominion University Archives.)

William and Mary was not the first institution in Hampton Roads to have student-led LGBT clubs, but it was the first to have an alumni association for gays and lesbians. Spanish professor George Greenia was key in breaking through on the conservative campus. (Courtesy of Wikimedia.)

In 1987, under direct orders from the Vatican, Bishop Walter Sullivan prevented a local Dignity chapter for gay Catholics from meeting at Sacred Heart Church in Norfolk. This decision led to Sacred Heart's priest leaving the priesthood and the area. (Courtesy of the Sargeant Memorial Room at Norfolk Public Library.)

Pictured here are now-prominent florists Laurel Quarberg (left) and Sarah Munford shortly after their first date in 1987. Their community engagement began with the civic league in Ingleside, and that penchant followed them to their home in Larchmont. They recently married in San Francisco, California, and Laurel served as president of the board of Hampton Roads Pride. (Courtesy of Laurel Quarberg.)

41

Pictured here is a group of gay amateur volleyball players at Stockley Gardens in Norfolk's Ghent neighborhood in 1986. Ghent's revitalization drew many young adults—both gay and straight—to the former streetcar suburb. As middle-class families left Norfolk because of public school desegregation, singles of all orientations took their place. (Courtesy of Fred Osgood.)

Informal volleyball games were just one of many sports outlets for LGBT people in the Hampton Roads area during the 1980s. Softball and bowling tournaments and competitions were also held. Formal leagues, separated by gender, appeared in the next decade. (Courtesy of Fred Osgood.)

Four

TRIUMPH AND TRAGEDY
ENDURING THE PLAGUE YEARS,
1988–1998

The HIV/AIDS epidemic affected Hampton Roads from its very beginnings in 1981, but its greatest local toll took place in the late 1980s and 1990s. Leaders such as Joseph McKay of the Unitarian church as well as psychiatrist Dr. Robert Scott were some of the first to die of this plague, which seemed to sap some of the activist energy that had been building in the previous decade. Nevertheless, the region provided a robust response to help those infected and affected by the disease. By 1998, Hampton Roads featured six AIDS service organizations (ASOs): Tidewater AIDS Crisis Taskforce (TACT), Candii House, Full Circle, Peninsula AIDS Foundation (PAF), Urban League, and the Williamsburg AIDS Network (WAN). TACT had been the first regional response to the epidemic, having been born in 1983. It would absorb the AIDS Health and Education Fund in 1988. PAF would be launched by TACT supporters in 1987, followed by Candii House in 1988 and the Full Circle Hospice in 1991. TACT and, to a lesser extent, PAF had many roots in the bar and club scene; Candii House and Full Circle had much more of a religious founding. Fragmentation became a problem, and self-inflicted wounds also diverted needed funds. In January 1993, TACT's executive director left town with over $27,600 in AIDSWalk monies and did not come back until caught by the police, forever crippling the agency's image with its stakeholders. Yet Alicia Devine, Dr. Robert Scott's daughter, and health care administrator James Spivey, among others, worked tirelessly to do damage control in the wake of this scandal and revive TACT, which remained the region's oldest and largest ASO at the end of the century.

In the midst of this pain and suffering, Hampton Roads established its annual Pride celebrations. Forerunners of what became known as Hampton Roads Pride were held as early as 1981, but the first annual "Out in the Park" Gay Pride Picnic was sponsored and organized by members of the Mandamus Society in July 1989 at Norfolk's Northside Community Park. The very next year, a coalition of various gay and lesbian organizations and interests was formed to organize future pride events: the Hampton Roads Lesbian and Gay Pride Coalition.

ROBERT, NANCY, BEN, JOHN, PAUL, SCOTT, PHIL, SAMUEL, SUE, TOM, SID,
JOE, TAMMY, MICHAEL, JEFF, MARK, TIM, MIKE, DENNIS, HAROLD, BOB,
PAULA, WAYNE, MARCUS, JIM, BILL, JOSEPH, MARCY, ELAINE, CHRIS,
RON, CORRIN, CASSEY, JAKOB, GEROME, ROB, ANITA, ED, ROBBY, ERICA,
MARY, EDWARD, CLARK, FRANK, STEVE, JOAN, PAT, KATE, JOYCE, LANCE,

HOPE, LOVE,
SHIRLEY, THOMAS, WREN,
MIKE, ARNIE, ART,
BRENT, LILY, BRIAN, ALTON, HELEN, APRIL, GEORGE, JENNA, PAM, J.R.,
DAVE, BRENT
BO,
CORWIN,
UCK,
B.J., DOLLY
BIE,
WE REMEMBER
MARRIE, ROBERT, NANCY, BEN, JOHN, PAUL, SCOTT, PHIL, SAMUEL, SUE,
TOM, SID, TAMMY, MICHAEL, MARK, TIM, MIKE, DENNIS, BOB,
MARCUS, MARCY, ELAINE, CHRIS,
DON'T CASSEY, TA, ED, ROBBY, ERICA,
SAY YOU WARD, CLA, KATE, CE,
GRANT, BU, Y, THOMAS, WREN,
SUSAN, STEPHEN, MIKE, ARNIE, ART,
BR **CARE** BR, R.,
DAVE, BRENT SA, SSA, DIANN, BO,
SHOW YOU CARE!
BE SAFE

HELP US HELP THOSE

WE NEED
VOLUNTEERS TO ...
BE A BUDDY,
DO PHONE WORK,
TRANSPORTATION,
SUPPORT, ETC.
CALL:
423-5859   **T.A.C.T.**
PENINSULA   814 WEST 41st STREET
877-1300   NORFOLK, VA. 23508

IN NEED - VOLUNTEER

This advertisement for the Tidewater AIDS Crisis Taskforce is poignant in that it features the names of people who had died of HIV/AIDS in the manner of the recently built Vietnam Veterans Memorial in Washington, DC. Local quilts were also made to commemorate the suddenly fallen. (Courtesy of the Old Dominion University Archives.)

Volunteers were especially necessary during the early days of the AIDS epidemic to provide solace for those who had no hope. Buddies provided home and hospice care, while others fought stigma and red tape to bring the latest remedies to the region. (Courtesy of the Old Dominion University Archives.)

While the Tidewater AIDS Crisis
Taskforce concentrated its early efforts
on the case management of people
who already had HIV/AIDS, the AIDS
Housing Education Fund focused its
activity on prevention and housing. Early
drugs to combat the disease proved to
be toxic to many, however, and stigma
and prejudice interfered with initial
prevention efforts. (Courtesy of the
Old Dominion University Archives.)

Fragmentation rather than consolidation tended to be the trend for local AIDS service organizations,
but there were successful attempts at unity. For instance, Mary Ann Moore, executive director
of Tidewater AIDS Crisis Taskforce (TACT), and John Picot, acting director of AIDS Housing
and Education Fund (AHEF), are pictured here at the August 11, 1988, reception marking the
merger of the two groups. (Courtesy of the Old Dominion University Archives.)

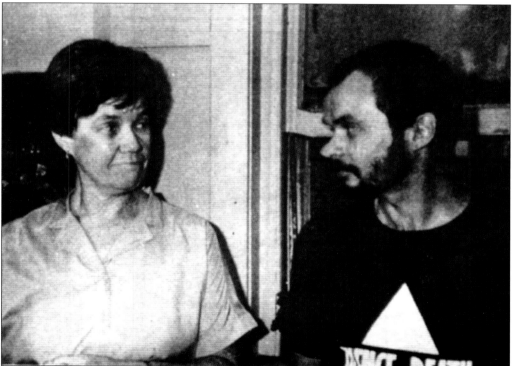

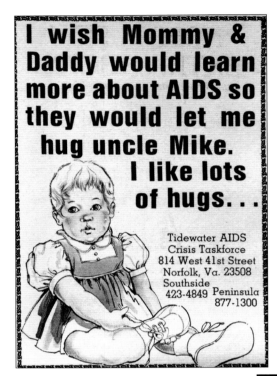

I wish Mommy & Daddy would learn more about AIDS so they would let me hug uncle Mike. I like lots of hugs...

Tidewater AIDS Crisis Taskforce
814 West 41st Street
Norfolk, Va. 23508
Southside
423-4849 Peninsula
877-1300

In the early days of the AIDS epidemic, there were so many irrational fears; no one knew how the disease was spread. As clinicians learned more, it was important for the public to understand how the HIV virus was transmitted. This advertisement tries to dispel ideas that casual contact could impart HIV. (Courtesy of the Old Dominion University Archives.)

Psychiatrist Robert Scott was a voice for equal rights. A cofounder of the Mandamus Society in 1981, he warns about the perils of HIV/AIDS in a 1982 article, "AIDS: History and Outlook." In 1983, he joined Tony Pritchard, Henry Garden, Ed Jones, and Sallie Jones to found the AIDS Fund, which became the Tidewater AIDS Crisis Taskforce in 1985. Scott died in 1988. (Courtesy of the Old Dominion University Archives.)

An Alternative...

The Mandamus Society offers a wide variety of social, cultural and educational activities, including dances, pot lucks, benefits for gay causes, picnics, speakers, and an annual harbor moonlight dance cruise.

For information about events or membership, call 622-6220 or write TMS, P.O. Box 411, Norfolk, VA 23501

Friendship Day Potluck Picnic
1 PM - 6 PM June 22
Northwest River Park, Chesapeake, VA

Moonlight Harbor Cruise
August 22

This is an advertisement for a forerunner of today's Hampton Roads Pride Festival. The Mandamus Society supported all kinds of civil liberties causes in the 1980s, but its primary focus was gay rights. It was also a key founder of the Tidewater AIDS Crisis Taskforce in 1983. (Courtesy of the Old Dominion University Archives.)

One of the most popular sites for the early Hampton Roads Pride Festivals was Virginia Beach's Mount Trashmore, which was a man-made mountain literally built on a landfill. The space was perhaps too big for the crowds and vendors in these years; the attendance seemed to decrease by the turn of the century. (Courtesy of Mel Frizzell.)

Pictured here are Mel Frizzell (right) and an unidentified friend. Mel was a student leader in the LGBT club at Old Dominion University, ODU Out, which had been founded a decade before. The club seemed to go dormant in the 1980s, as the cultural conservatism of the Reagan era took hold. Yet by the end of the decade, it began organizing and agitating once again. (Courtesy of Mel Frizzell.)

Student leaders at Old Dominion got a big boost from above in the early 1990s. The new university president, James Koch, set an inclusive tone and implemented LGBT-friendly policies almost right after he was inaugurated. For example, he established a liaison for LGBT issues in the student affairs division. (Courtesy of Mel Frizzell.)

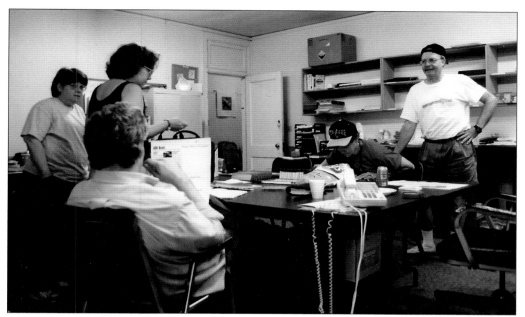

Pictured here are *Our Own Community Press* staff members in 1997 as they work toward meeting a deadline. *Our Own Community Press* remained the main LGBT voice in Hampton Roads for only just another year, but Henry Edgar's newsletter *Out and About* supplemented its coverage of bar events and nightlife. (Courtesy of Fred Osgood.)

Pictured here is a staff member of *Our Own Community Press*, choosing which books and materials to review. The newspaper maintained a robust book review section to raise awareness and identity among its readers. Its titular owners, Jim Early and his partner Garland Tillery, were determined to keep Hampton Roads aware of the latest intellectual and cultural happenings. (Courtesy of Fred Osgood.)

In the last years of *Our Own Community Press*, editor Kirk Read and publisher Alicia Herr used computers to lay out and edit the newspaper's content. More importantly, they successfully tried to balance content and coverage between gay male and lesbian stories. Earlier editions had been accused of being too partial to either men or women. (Courtesy of Fred Osgood.)

Editorial decisions could be quite controversial at *Our Own*. For example, the paper continued to run telephone-sex advertisements for interested gay men, even though many readers—mainly lesbians—objected to the prurient nature of the ads. But for budget reasons, the paper had no choice but to run those and other advertisements. (Courtesy of Fred Osgood.)

Pictured here is a military couple just back from Desert Storm who were part of a protest over military oppression of gay and lesbian service members at the naval base in June 1991. The first Iraq War underscored the paradox of servicemen and women fighting for freedom yet being unable to be truly free themselves. (Courtesy of the *Virginian-Pilot* Archives.)

Tracy Thorne joined the US Navy in 1988, and moved to Virginia Beach. In 1992, he came out on ABC's *Nightline*, sparking the Navy's effort to get rid of him. After being honorably discharged in 1995, Thorne lost his suit to be reinstated. Later, in 2013, he became the first openly gay person to be confirmed to serve on the 13th District Court in Richmond. (Courtesy of the *Washington Post*.)

51

As the 1990s dawned, there was a burst of activism among young gay and lesbian students, which was not matched by political change. This feature article in the *Virginian-Pilot* looks at local young people caught in this bind. It also details the activities of Youth Out United, which was formed by these young people themselves. (Courtesy of the *Virginian-Pilot*.)

As soon as he became university president in the early 1990s, James Koch opened up Old Dominion University to many minority groups in order for the institution to grow, and LGBT folks were no exception. For example, Koch appointed a special liaison to gays and lesbians, and he cracked down on instances of campus bigotry. (Courtesy of the Old Dominion University Archives.)

In 1991, the Gay Men's Book Group of Hampton Roads formed to provide an alternative to the bar scene for middle-aged and middle-class men. It has met at a member's house every third Sunday to discuss one book ever since. Pictured here are longtime members Tony Crudup (left), Don Martin (center), and Ken Orr. (Courtesy of Charles H. Ford.)

Sharon Bottoms was sued by her own mother, Kay, for custody of her son Tyler in 1993 because Sharon was living with her partner April Wade. Virginia Circuit Court judge Buford M. Parsons awarded custody to the grandmother because Sharon was deemed inherently criminal as an out-and-proud lesbian. That next year, an appeals court reversed this travesty of justice, but the Virginia Supreme Court ultimately upheld Parsons's notorious decision. (Courtesy of the Advocate.)

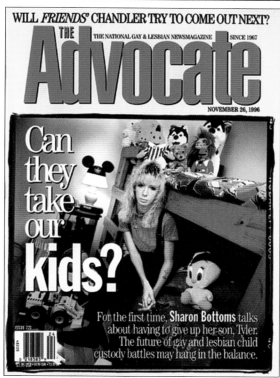

WILL *FRIENDS'* CHANDLER TRY TO COME OUT NEXT?

The Advocate

THE NATIONAL GAY & LESBIAN NEWSMAGAZINE   SINCE 1967

NOVEMBER 26, 1996

Can they take our kids?

For the first time, **Sharon Bottoms** talks about having to give up her son, Tyler. The future of gay and lesbian child custody battles may hang in the balance.

The Knight Hawks formed in 1994 to provide a social club for those interested in the leather and Levis subculture. The Knight Hawks do all kinds of charity work; a member is pictured here bringing donations for a children's benefit. (Courtesy of the Knight Hawks.)

Leisa Meyer, professor of history at William and Mary, was instrumental in bringing the first SAFE zones to campus in eastern Virginia. SAFE zones are designed to indicate which faculty and staff members are open to the full inclusion of sexual minorities. (Courtesy of the National Women's History Museum.)

Five

TREADING WATER
IN TRANSITION
OUR OWN AFTER OUR OWN
COMMUNITY PRESS, 1998–2007

At the turn of the 21st century, LGBT Hampton Roads seemed to be going backward rather than forward. *Our Own Community Press* closed suddenly in 1998, and the region was left without that important local voice for advocacy. Pride celebrations attracted relatively few attendees and patrons, despite the efforts of their organizers. The military's embrace of "Don't ask, don't tell" continued to force thousands of servicemen and women stationed at the array of bases here to remain in the closet. The US Supreme Court's 2003 invalidation of state sodomy laws with *Lawrence v. Texas* was certainly welcomed here, but marriage equality seemed unattainable with the codification of discrimination in 2004 by the Virginia General Assembly. Indeed, after courts gave the go-ahead to same-sex unions in liberal New England, the fight for marriage equality in the new century quickly turned to the arenas of state legislatures and referenda. In Virginia, one of the most socially conservative states in the union, the Marshall-Newman Amendment of 2006 enshrined in the Old Dominion's Constitution an especially restrictive response, putting fundamental human rights up to a simple majority vote. In Hampton Roads, a broad-based coalition of progressives led by Equality Virginia actively opposed it, helping to narrow the margin of victory statewide for the Religious Right.

The outlook for other LGBT-founded infrastructure appeared mixed at best in this period. In particular, the region's ASOs were forced to consolidate, as improving diagnoses and outlooks for patients drew community interest elsewhere. Weekly bingo games and government grants provided their lifeline of support. PAF went out of business in 2002, and its clients on the Lower Peninsula were helped by its sister agencies on the south side. Candii House and Full Circle united in 2005 to form Access AIDS Care, which remains the region's only ASO a decade later.

While formerly active LGBT student organizations at Old Dominion University remained relatively dormant during this period, there were promising signs elsewhere. At Norfolk State University, the region's historically African American public institution of higher learning, Leading the Education of Gay and Straight Individuals (LEGASI) received official status as a campus club in 2004.

Lambda Rising bookstores, an LGBT-focused chain launched by Washingtonian activist Deacon Maccubbin in 1974, were essential pillars of communities in the Mid-Atlantic until the Washington anchor store closed in 2010. At its peak at the turn of the century, the chain featured four stores—Washington, Baltimore, Rehoboth Beach, and Norfolk. They provided safe spaces to shop for the latest literary works by and about LGBT people. (Courtesy of Barry Moore.)

Beautician and activist Mitch Rosa witnessed the Stonewall rebellion as a child in New York City in 1969. The US Navy brought Rosa to Norfolk, and he never left. The epitome of a grassroots organizer, Rosa helped keep key community institutions such as the Hampton Roads Gay and Lesbian Pride Coalition as well as the Tidewater AIDS Crisis Taskforce going for decades. (Courtesy of Barry Moore.)

In 2003, the US Supreme Court struck down state sodomy statutes nationwide in *Lawrence v. Texas*, and the following year Massachusetts approved same-sex marriages. In Virginia, however, legislators passed House Bill 751 to define marriage as a union between one man and one woman. The LGBT activists pictured here are protesting the Virginia law at Norfolk's Waterside on the evening of June 30, 2004. (Courtesy of Kiley Pike.)

The protests pictured here were unsuccessful in the short-term because further court action inspired the constitutional referendum of 2006, which placed marriage inequality in the Virginia Constitution. In Hampton Roads, however, support for gay marriage helped to make the winning percentage of the Marshall-Newman Amendment only 52 percent statewide. (Courtesy of Kiley Pike.)

Suddenly, in the summer of 2004, Congressman Ed Schrock of Norfolk resigned. A blogger had come out to say that Schrock had been trying to solicit sex from young men. This was very surprising for the married, ostensibly heterosexual former Navy commander. (Courtesy of Wikimedia.)

Attorney Joseph Price, a former Tidewater resident and frequent visitor to the region in these years, was instrumental in the transformation of the amateurish Virginians for Justice into the more professional Equality Virginia. That success was eclipsed suddenly by the murder of his friend and fellow attorney Robert Wone in his Washington, DC, home in August 2006. Price and his partner Victor Zaborsky and their friend Dylan Ward were indicted for obstructing justice in the murder investigation, but they were eventually acquitted. (Courtesy of the *Washington Post*.)

Here are members of the Rainbow Riders Cycling Club providing information about their activities to passersby at the 2003 Hampton Roads PrideFest. The event was held in Lakewood Park in Norfolk. (Courtesy of Barry Moore.)

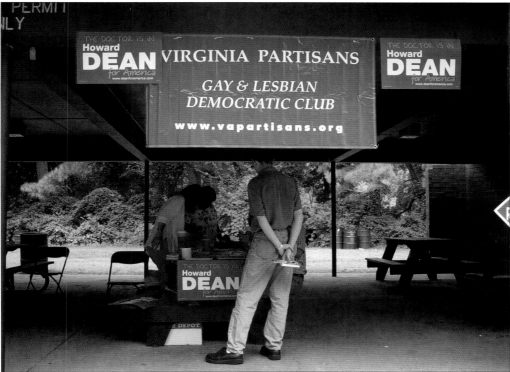

In 2003, the Democratic Party's LGBT wing in the state was still known as the Virginia Partisans, who seem to be here gravitating toward the insurgent candidacy of Howard Dean largely because his home state of Vermont had already allowed some kind of marriage equality. (Courtesy of Barry Moore.)

Voter registration was an important part of Prides, even though the attendance and logistical follow-through were never what the organizers had expected. (Courtesy of Barry Moore.)

The local park venues selected for Pride events in the first years of the century seem to have been out of the way and hidden, reflecting perhaps the anxieties and tentativeness of their participants. (Courtesy of Barry Moore.)

Here, Diana Ross, an established drag performer in Hampton Roads, is doing a particularly upbeat number for the crowd. (Courtesy of Barry Moore.)

The local lesbian band Mermaids in the Basement often performed at Pride events during the early years of the 21st century. Big headliners would have to wait for the next decade. (Courtesy of Barry Moore.)

Vendors of all kinds participated in PrideFest during these years, even if there was no separate section for children and families to enjoy. (Courtesy of Barry Moore.)

Despite official characterizations of LGBT folk as elite, white, and male, this photograph shows the sociological diversity of the communities. That diversity was not always reflected in the leadership of local organizations, however. (Courtesy of Barry Moore.)

Barry Moore's *Lambda Directory* has long been the Bible for locating friendly businesses. Before Hampton Roads Business Outreach (HRBOR), it was the only way for like-minded shop owners and consumers to reach one another. (Courtesy of Barry Moore.)

In 2006, drag performer Diana Ross appears at PrideFest in an especially dramatic gown. This photograph captures the energy and passion that went into this act. She has been performing locally since the early 1970s, outlasting many of her contemporaries on the stage. (Courtesy of Barry Moore.)

The centrality of the rainbow flag in this photograph seems to be the anchor for the sometimes bewildering diversity of LGBT communities. The scattering of people around the flag in this Chesapeake park is symbolic of the problems faced by local LGBT communities in this era of transition. (Courtesy of Barry Moore.)

A Caribbean-themed dancing act at PrideFest in 2006 underscored not only the maritime nature of the region but also its cultural diversity and transatlantic ties as well. (Courtesy of Barry Moore.)

Accountant and open lesbian Vivian J. Paige (right) ran to be Norfolk treasurer in 2005, only to have a whispering campaign about her orientation cost her the victory in the municipal election. Paige went on to put forth a well-regarded blog on civic and political matters. She is pictured in this undated photograph with Hillary Clinton. (Courtesy of Vivian J. Paige.)

In April 2005, a summit of state LGBT leaders at Virginia Commonwealth University—which included history professor and coauthor Charles H. Ford of Norfolk State University—drafted a grant proposal to the Ford Foundation's Difficult Dialogues competition. Out of this effort came Network Virginia, which was designed to connect leaders on Virginia's college campuses in order to stimulate change on LGBT issues. (Courtesy of Network Virginia.)

One of the founders of Network Virginia was social work professor Elizabeth Cramer, who later collaborated with future coauthor of this book Charles Ford of Norfolk State to help to build one of the first intercampus faculty learning communities in the country on fighting oppression in the classroom. This connected faculty at Cramer's Virginia Commonwealth and Ford's Norfolk State Universities to discuss LGBT issues, among other things. (Courtesy of Liz Cramer.)

Six

RENAISSANCE AND TRANSFORMATION IN THE NEW CENTURY
2007–2015

The latest renaissance of the cultures of LGBT Hampton Roads began with attorney and blogger Michael Hamar sitting down with friends to discuss mutually beneficial collaborations. The result of these discussions was Hampton Roads Business Outreach (HRBOR), which first met at Norfolk's Town Point Club in June 2007. Since its inception, HRBOR has helped to dispel the isolation and bickering that had previously held back local LGBT businesses, organizations, and individuals from helping each other to reach their highest potential.

A quantum leap in the visibility and influence of LGBT Hampton Roads occurred with the moving of PrideFest to the conventional showcase of Norfolk's Town Point Park in June 2011. This daring gamble permanently enhanced the funding and logistics for the event and has brought the communities much closer to both civic and state officials. Key in this transformation were straight allies such as Jesse Scaccia, the then editor of *AltDaily*, and mortgage broker Cindy Cutler, among others. Together with local LGBT leaders such as nurse James Hermansen-Parker, the Virginia Stage Company's Patrick Mullins, banker Kathleen Blevins, and auditor Michael Beane, among others, they convinced Hampton Roads Business Outreach (HRBOR), the LGBT Chamber of Commerce, of its viability. This then enabled the cultivation of larger donors and better vendors, which, in turn, allowed for much more ambitious and complex extravaganzas than ever before, despite bouts of bad weather. Pride has become Norfolk's second-biggest overall event in terms of size and attendance and features the only boat parade for a Pride event in North America; only Amsterdam does another one worldwide.

Other collaborations have been just as amazing. For instance, a group of determined local faculty members spearheaded by Drs. Dana Heller and Avi Santo of Old Dominion University and community leaders wanted to bring LGBT studies to the area. Usually, that kind of programming and coursework is found only at elite or Northern institutions, but they and their collaborators from Norfolk State and Christopher Newport Universities thought that it was important to offer such curricular fare to working-class Virginia. Accordingly, in July 2010, they formally launched the Old Dominion Gay Cultural Studies Endowment campaign.

Pictured here are founder and soon-to-be president of Hampton Roads Business Outreach (HRBOR) Carl Johansen and Norfolk State student Andre Christian at the monthly HRBOR meeting in September 2013, this time held at Norfolk State's new Brooks Library. HRBOR has mentored young leaders at all of the region's colleges. (Courtesy of HRBOR.)

This picture was taken in August 2015 at the monthly HRBOR networking meeting, which was held at the Chrysler Museum of Art in conjunction with Hampton Roads Pride. This event kicked off an art exhibit with the added punch of good attendance from the combined efforts of several organizations. (Courtesy of HRBOR.)

This December 2011 photograph was taken at the monthly HRBOR networking meeting, which occurred at the former Chamberlin Hotel in Hampton. HRBOR has had two meetings per year on the Lower Peninsula and has been invited to become a member of the prestigious Peninsula Chamber of Commerce. (Courtesy of HRBOR.)

This photograph was taken in July 2015 at the monthly HRBOR networking meeting; pictured here, among others, are power couple Chris Vaigneur (left) and Carlton Hardy (second from left). In particular, Carlton has been active in the leadership of area cultural organizations, and HRBOR has been a benefit to him and others in overcoming regional and institutional obstacles to connection and communication. (Courtesy of HRBOR.)

Pictured here are HRBOR members, from left to right, Staci Walls-Beegle of ACCESS AIDS Care, nurse James Hermansen-Parker from Hampton Roads Pride, and realtor Don King, then president of HRBOR. They are awaiting President Obama's visit to Langley Air Force Base in 2012. State and local politicians have become regular guests at HRBOR meetings, as the influence of a relatively united front has begun to take shape. (Courtesy of HRBOR.)

Here, Todd Rosenlieb of TR Dance eagerly awaits the program of the monthly HRBOR networking event in 2012 at 757 Creative Space. Arts and cultural organizations have definitely benefited from these community and business gatherings. (Courtesy of HRBOR.)

This HRBOR meeting was held in Hampton at the Tysinger Motor Company, a leading regional car dealership since 1926. The participation of such community pillars in HRBOR has greatly enhanced the credibility, scope, and success of other LGBT events and organizations in the area. (Courtesy of HRBOR.)

Pictured here are mortgage brokers Randy DeMille and Cindy Cutler; both are stalwart HRBOR members. Cutler also was a key straight ally in the making of HRBOR and the bringing of Hampton Roads PrideFest to Norfolk's Town Point Park in 2011. (Courtesy of HRBOR.)

Pictured here are food critic Patrick Evans-Hylton (left) and his partner and now husband, Wayne Hylton, at a HRBOR event in February 2011. A generation before, Patrick served on the staff of *Our Own Community Press* and helped to launch the Hampton Roads cohort of Queer Nation. (Courtesy of HRBOR.)

Pictured here are ACCESS AIDS Care's Staci Walls-Beegle and federal administrator Bill Calvert at a monthly HRBOR networking meeting. One of the by-products of ACCESS AIDS Care's involvement with HRBOR has been its successful launch of the region's first LGBT community center in Norfolk's Park Place. In 1985, area bar owners had wanted to open a similar center, but intermural fighting precluded any such opening. (Courtesy of HRBOR.)

Since 2010, Old Dominion University's gay cultural studies has sponsored events featuring top filmmakers, academic speakers, and photographic exhibits for the public. The organization has also partnered with groups at its sister institutions in the region (such as Norfolk State and Christopher Newport Universities). Its board continues to hope that student demand, paired with community support, will bring experts in this field to Hampton Roads. (Courtesy of Barry Moore.)

The Human Rights Campaign (HRC) has always maintained a presence at Hampton Roads PrideFest, and 2011 was no exception. Enthusiasm for its legal and political victories has led to the assembling of at least two Hampton Roads delegations in subsequent years to HRC's annual dinner in Washington, DC. (Courtesy of Barry Moore.)

Part of the increased visibility of Hampton Roads Pride has been its advertising in conventional places, such as the marquee outside of Norfolk's Nauticus museum. Another favorite spot for Pride advertisements has been on the outer shell of the light-rail cars connecting the eastern part of the city with its downtown. (Courtesy of Barry Moore.)

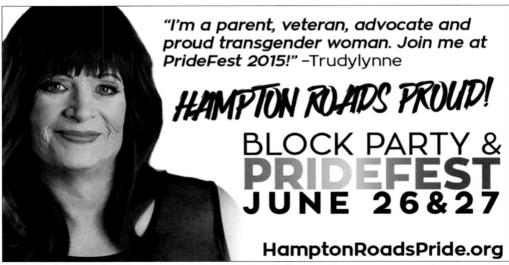

In 2015, the Board of Hampton Roads Pride decided to emphasize its support for transgender issues. Trudylynne O'Brien, pictured on this billboard, became the de facto face of the event in order to underscore this priority. (Courtesy of Hampton Roads Pride.)

Pictured here are Pride members Cole Werkheiser (left) and Michael Berlucchi at the 2014 Interfaith Celebration, a key component of the weeklong series of events leading up to the PrideFest that year. This one was held at the Metropolitan Community Church in Norfolk's Norview neighborhood. (Courtesy of Hampton Roads Pride.)

The annual block party has become an extravaganza in itself. Originally conceived in 2012 as a prelude to PrideFest, it has grown to rival in size and scope its originating event. Bad weather in 2015 moved it to Norfolk's Scope, ironically the same venue in which antigay activist Anita Bryant had performed 38 years previously. (Courtesy of Hampton Roads Pride.)

The LGBT Center of Hampton Roads sponsored a tent and advertised its own programming at the 2013 PrideFest. The LGBT Center is located on Twenty-fifth Street in Norfolk's Park Place, and it is a component of ACCESS AIDS Care. (Courtesy of Barry Moore.)

The PrideFest featured wedding officiants even before the Supreme Court ruled that gay marriage was legal in 2015. Pictured here in 2011 is a representative of the Holy Union Wedding Chapel of Norfolk, Virginia. In 2014, the Reverend Mark Byrd of the local Metropolitan Community Church organized an entire section of the park to concentrate on marriage equality. (Courtesy of Barry Moore.)

This great vista underscores the importance of moving the festival to center stage at Town Point Park in Norfolk. The event has become the second-largest in the city's calendar, surpassed by only Harborfest. (Courtesy of Barry Moore.)

The musical and dance acts at PrideFest have continued to diversify. Here, country-and-western artists are featured in 2011, and in 2015 a Marine band actually performed. (Courtesy of Barry Moore.)

Drag acts have not been forgotten in this drive to make the community more assimilated. If anything, drag acts have been celebrated and placed on center stage by the organizers. (Courtesy of Barry Moore.)

Veteran bar owner Annette Stone (center) is pictured here at PrideFest with friends. Bar owners, like drag acts, have not been forgotten in the drive for respectability and acceptance. (Courtesy of Barry Moore.)

Pictured here are Rock Victorian (left), Tony Wagerman (center), and J. Clay McNutt at the 2011 Hampton Roads PrideFest. The group was photographed in front of Norfolk's Waterside, which has since been closed and slated for possible redevelopment. (Courtesy of Tony Wagerman.)

Pictured here are Shannon Bowman and Jimmy Biascan, who helped market Pride as it moved to Town Point Park. (Courtesy of Tony Wagerman.)

ODU undergraduate Connor Norton (left) is pictured here with an unidentified friend. Connor was a key student leader in getting the support of young people for LGBT events and organizations in Hampton Roads. He helped to produce a play that dramatized the passage of Proposition 8 in California, a referendum that temporarily nullified marriage equality in that state. (Courtesy of Tony Wagerman.)

This photograph demonstrates the diversity and size of the crowd that braved the hot temperatures at the 2013 PrideFest at Town Point Park. (Courtesy of Barry Moore.)

One of the biggest supporters of Hampton Roads Pride since its move to Town Point Park has been Decorum Furniture. Pictured here are its employees with a vending tent. (Courtesy of Barry Moore.)

One of the distinctive aspects of Hampton Roads Pride since 2011 has been its boat parade up and down the Elizabeth River. Here is the entry sponsored by Tidewater Home Funding in 2013. (Courtesy of Barry Moore.)

The boat parade has been a publicity success because it draws upon the region's maritime nature. Here the entrants express their approval of the Supreme Court's 2013 decision in the Windsor case in a whimsical way. (Courtesy of Barry Moore.)

ACCESS AIDS Care has not been forgotten, even though the face and nature of AIDS has changed in the last generation. Free HIV testing has been offered at Pride events. (Courtesy of Barry Moore.)

The organization of PrideFest has been a mammoth effort requiring a legion of volunteers and the cooperation of local businesses. Distinctive Events Rentals has been especially helpful in providing logistical support for the event. (Courtesy of Barry Moore.)

Barry Moore has kept the *Lambda Directory* going in the digital age and has provided the *Lambda Voice* as a partial substitute for *Our Own Community Press*. (Courtesy of Barry Moore.)

Center stage has featured national divas such as Deborah Cox in 2014 and regional artists like Tom Goss in 2013. (Courtesy of Barry Moore.)

Mermaids in the Basement, a local lesbian band since the 1980s, reunites here in 2013 to provide a trip down memory lane. (Courtesy of Barry Moore.)

The Prime Timers of Southeastern Virginia are geared toward senior-citizen gay men and their friends. Here, they sponsor a booth at the 2013 PrideFest. (Courtesy of Barry Moore.)

The Unitarians, while not as prominent or powerful as they were in the 1970s and 1980s, still maintain a booth at PrideFest. Their universal approach to social justice is actually more relevant today that it has ever been before. (Courtesy of Barry Moore.)

Business support has been key in the success of these recent PrideFests, and defense consultant Booz Allen Hamilton has been right at the center of these collaborative efforts. (Courtesy of Barry Moore.)

Local singer Narissa Bond provides a moment of folk music before the more usual fare of techno and disco at the 2013 PrideFest in Town Point Park. (Courtesy of Barry Moore.)

Lt. Gov. Ralph Northam is pictured here addressing the crowd at PrideFest in June 2015. State and municipal support of the event has grown dramatically with its increasing scope and attendance. (Courtesy of Hampton Roads Pride.)

Activist Cleve Jones first thought of doing a quilt to commemorate people who had died of AIDS in 1985. Two years later, commemorative panels were made, and the first display of all of the panels on the National Mall in Washington, DC, happened in 1987. Here, as part of Hampton Roads Pride's History Experience in June 2015, four panels of the AIDS Quilt are displayed. (Courtesy of Charles H. Ford.)

One of the most enjoyable parts of the recent PrideFest has been the participation of the tall ship *American Rover*. The *Rover* has led the boat parade down the Elizabeth River and hosted a bevy of local celebrities and politicians to further enhance the profile of the event. Pictured here is a couple enjoying the views and company on board. (Courtesy of Charles H. Ford.)

Pictured here are, from left to right, J. Clay McNutt, Michael Hamar, Barry Menser, Cindy Cutler, Charles Stanton, and Diane Kaufman aboard the tall ship *American Rover* leading the boat parade for Hampton Roads Pride 2015. The convivial atmosphere on board foreshadows the delights on land. (Courtesy of Charles H. Ford.)

Here are members of the Reel-It-Out Queer Film Festival committee awarding the winner of their short films competition in 2013 at Old Dominion's University Theater. Pictured, from left to right, are committee members Chadra Pittman-Walke and Carlton Hardy along with prizewinner Antonio Caballero Gardyn. (Courtesy of Charles H. Ford.)

The first LGBT Film Festival in Hampton Roads was held at the iconic Naro Theater in Ghent during the early 1990s. In more recent times, the annual Reel-It-Out Queer Film Festival, begun in March 2013, screens films in six different locations around the region. Three universities—Old Dominion, Norfolk State, and Christopher Newport—and their LGBT student groups have contributed to and guided the programming. (Courtesy of Charles H. Ford.)

One of the strengths of the Reel-It-Out Queer Film Festival has been its screening of different films around the region. Here are patrons and volunteers after the showing of the documentary *Brother Outsider* in February 2014 at Norfolk State University, the area's largest historically African American public university. (Courtesy of Charles H. Ford.)

The local chapter of Parents and Friends of Lesbians and Gays (PFLAG) emerged from the Norfolk Unitarian Church under the leadership of parent and ally Patricia Metzler in the mid-1990s. The chapter has become quite active; here, members Brandon Brinkley (left) and David Dorbad are participating in a pro–marriage equality demonstration. (Courtesy of PFLAG, Norfolk/South Hampton Roads.)

From 2006 to 2014, Hampton Roads leaders hosted an event to honor their own for Equality Virginia. In 2011, the event—Equality Virginia Legends—was held in Virginia Beach and had a Parisian theme, as evidenced by the poster. (Courtesy of Jimmy Biascan.)

Here are three local legends together at Equality Virginia's Legends Gala held at the then Norfolk Plaza Hotel in November 2012. From left to right are Carlton Hardy, Ann Vernon, and Bill Griggs. (Courtesy of Carlton Hardy.)

Ever since Virginians for Justice became Equality Virginia in 2002, there has been a lobby day for LGBT constituents to meet their representatives in Richmond. Constituents from Hampton Roads—from left to right, Tony Wagerman, Sarah Bell Murphy, and Paul Meadors—are pictured here in February 2014 ready to do battle. (Courtesy of Charles H. Ford.)

In this March 2013 photograph taken outside the Walter E. Hoffman Courthouse, local leaders hold a vigil for marriage equality, hoping for a favorable decision from district court judge Arenda Wright Allen. (Courtesy of Charles H. Ford.)

Tim Bostic (left) and Tony London, pictured here at their wedding in May 2015, were the victorious plaintiffs in the suit that brought marriage equality to Hampton Roads and Virginia in general. (Courtesy of Charles H. Ford.)

Tim and Tony's reception was held at the Harrison Opera House, where several prominent politicians, including the mayor and lieutenant governor, came by. Pictured here are, from left to right, coauthor Charles H. Ford, Ken Elks, and Cindy Cutler. (Courtesy of Charles H. Ford.)

Here is the joyous reaction in November 2011 after the Obama administration ended the policy of "Don't ask, don't tell," which had ruined so many military careers locally. This is from an impromptu celebration at Norfolk's Waterside. (Courtesy of the *Virginian-Pilot*.)

When Norfolk State University's Faith Fitzgerald first sought recognition for Leading the Education of Gay and Straight Individuals (LEGASI) in 2004, she had a hard time convincing administrators of its necessity. Yet ever since its debut, LEGASI has been one of the most active student organizations on campus. LEGASI has helped with the Reel-It-Out Queer Film Festival and provided volunteers for community events. Pictured here are LEGASI students at the White House in Washington. (Courtesy of Charles H. Ford.)

Full Circle embraced the "Dinner Is Served" fundraiser template in 1995, and its successor organization—ACCESS AIDS Care—continues to benefit from these type of grassroots events. This is from the holiday-themed Dinner Is Served hosted in early December 2012 by two male couples: financial advisor Gregg Smith and banker Troy Hodgdon and psychiatrist Frank Kirchner and columnist David Nicholson, at the Kirchner-Nicholsons' home in the Lafayette-Winona section of Norfolk. (Courtesy of Charles H. Ford.)

Former teacher Joel McDonald (right) was elected by a wide margin to the Virginia Beach School Board in 2013; he ran as an openly gay candidate and was instrumental in getting a nondiscrimination clause approved by the board in 2015. The man on the left is unidentified. (Courtesy of Joel McDonald.)

Discover Thousands of Local History Books Featuring Millions of Vintage Images

Arcadia Publishing, the leading local history publisher in the United States, is committed to making history accessible and meaningful through publishing books that celebrate and preserve the heritage of America's people and places.

Find more books like this at
www.arcadiapublishing.com

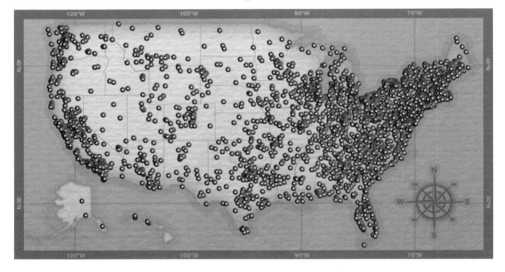

Search for your hometown history, your old stomping grounds, and even your favorite sports team.

Consistent with our mission to preserve history on a local level, this book was printed in South Carolina on American-made paper and manufactured entirely in the United States. Products carrying the accredited Forest Stewardship Council (FSC) label are printed on 100 percent FSC-certified paper.

MADE IN THE USA